The Internal Moon

Kasey Johnson

Presentation by *BookLeaf Publishing*

Web: www.bookleafpub.com

E-mail: info@bookleafpub.com

ISBN: 9789358737783

First edition 2023

ACKNOWLEDGEMENT

"The Human Spirit is stronger than anything that can happen to it."
- C.C. Scott

(P.S. There will always be infinity & beyond)

PREFACE

It is in the power of thought that we find our reality. Emotions are the groundwork for the path to be divided. The battle between mind and matter keeps insanity alive.

Trapped in Hope

Is that window cold?
That's what I've been told.
Hypocrisy will never make the devil fold.
Only an angel can be as bold.

Wrapped in love;
Spit out by stupor;
It really threw me for a loop, here.
Have faith in time and you'll rise above.

Clearly, gracious;
must be the patient.

How will everyone see you in the dark?
Will the shine show through?

Is it enough not to be seen, but just to leave a
mark?
Delinquent penance is due.

The darkness is universal.
Puppets afar stare in admiration.
Society prepares a rehearsal.
Are you the creator of inspiration?

If only they knew how you'd break.
Keep us close.
We are bound to awake.
Mind, body, & soul mingle in a polyphonic
prose.

Drag us behind..Let us be the eyes.
Every General has an army ready to fight.
Soldier or captain?
We can make it happen.

It may not be clear,
You know not of me, my dear.
Let me introduce myself: I am fear.

Ambition

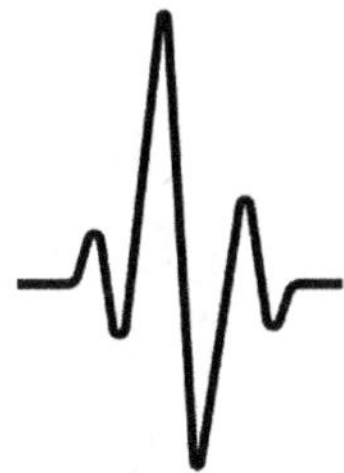

An urge of success,

Accomplished by innocence.

Prevail in knowledge.

Sunny Day?

I want to feel joy.

I want to smile in the sun!

Please don't forget me.

Manifesting Trance

Life is still.
Silence is real.
Peace has made a deal;
Time has lost its will.

The mind is now in control.
Feel the tranquility.
Release the wicked from your soul.
The future can be an acquired ability.

Dancing with Fire

I want so badly for you to understand;
You are the warrior kind of man.
I will always be your fan.
Confide in me, I promise that you can.

It is imperative I tell you my secret.
It's similar to Cleopatra in Egypt.
It becoming more and more frequent.
I can't help that love is my weakness...

You may lack the attention.

But lucky for me I like ambition.
Glad we could both be a part of the transition.
Maybe one day I will be able to listen.

Mr. Dedication

He dove in head first,
With an everlasting thirst.
A gift no longer the curse;
An ever-lasting passion ready to burst!

Light: Wide Open

A light in the dark,
Heed the warning to build the ark.
It is not us who will leave a mark,
But of the Gods' that love will spark.

Let go of the day-to-day.
It is not here we are to stay.
Is it the soul that prays?
For it will not be the substance that survives the
craze!

Clothe in silence.
Rid the world of violence.
Burden evil with defiance,
Build upon the divine alliance.

Share in peace,
in unison we breathe.

The conscious do not leave.
They will remain free.

Deep Horizons

If we lost it all tomorrow,
Would you share in the sorrow?

If a helping hand became needy,
Would you give to it freely?

If it stopped serving its purpose,
Would you find it worthless?

If it became routine,
Would you know the unseen?

If it stressed you out,
Would you start to doubt?

If your thoughts grew regretful,
Would intentions become forgetful?

Will you love the same,
If it did not change?

Will you tell the fortune,
If all you could speak is distortion?

Will it be of permanence,
Or is longevity purposeless?

Crazy Loon

This you is vain.
We can all still see your pain.
If only you'd wrap that around your brain. Your
memories are making us insane!

Look in the mirror...
You will see fear!
Let me hold you dear;
Give me the wheel to steer.

We all love you so,
Where did you go?
Be yourself, we are the only ones who will
know.
Something different from our usual show.

I hope I don't offend you,
But excuses give me the flu.
Ramble is all that you do!
It's okay, here, let US move...

Take it all over;
We expect no closure!
That game will make you a loner.
Deal us in on that game of poker.

A Long Road

I can't listen to music because it reminds me of
you.

The silence is real.
This is quiet...
I'm not fond of it.

I enjoyed the noise.
I enjoyed the laughter.

I am alone. I am alone.
I'm not strong enough to be.

Why didn't you try to stop me?
I shouldn't have done it.

Could we have come back from where we
allowed it to go?

It doesn't feel right.

Dear, Beautiful Woman…

When the hurt never ceases,
Do not live in shame.
You are HIS masterpiece,
So rejoice in love's flame.

If you get the feeling of guilt,
Do not follow the Trail of Tears.
Pain can be comfortably rebuilt,
Instant aid only enables our fears.

Let your soul be the gladiator!
The internal battle you will win.
Let Karma be the mediator,
You just heal & mend.

Vibe A Little

Freely breathe it in.

Vibrations strum emotions.

Enjoy the love here.

Edgy Ego(s)

Your narcissistic ways,
Crash into me like waves.
Insanity created a maze,
Trapped in a manifesting daze.

You make it hard.
I don't want you to stay.
You make it hard.
It doesn't have to be that way.
You make it hard.
It will haunt you someday.

A tightness grows inside,
Not in you, but in myself I must confide.
The tears rest on the lashes of my eyes,
Will fame make you feel alive?

You make it hard.
Telling the truth with lies.
You make it hard.
Please don't open my eyes.
You make it hard.
No need to say goodbye.

How can your infamy save us all?
In seclusion, guilt will stand tall.
Being so high will make it hard to catch us if we
fall.
Yesterday, we had everything! Do you not
recall?

You make it hard.
Don't go too far!
You make it hard.
We've just dealt the cards.
You make it hard.
If only I knew who you are…

Embrace the distance,
For I will inevitability fight the resistance.
Glory are your days of temperance?

Leave it to the past for remembrance.

Keep practicing, now you are learning…
While I have your attention let me explain the
yearning.
I mean as much as you, this I can say with
certainty.
Give it back, my love, I will cherish it for
eternity.

Let yourself be free...
Because I am through with you; inside of me.

Dear Silence

I will learn how to enjoy you.
I will figure out what you're about.
I used to long for the quiet, just a moment to
check my mood.
Though, I didn't want to go this route...

I always knew you could.
So I will learn to find my self in this empty
space.
Hey, ya know... It's all good.
It's certainly time for me to save some face.

Let the tick of the clock keep me focused,For I
can then find myself in the hollow.
God, we will miss those lovely moments.
But catch you on the slip side;
or at the temple of Apollo.

A Wrongful Escape

You erode the genuine.

Fooling to be a friend to them.

It's a battle no one wins!

A mission of life to live.

Always searching for the outlet.

Each high just a riskier bet!

The moments of righteousness don't pay the
debt.

For you are what we'll always regret.

Twin Flame

I am not sure if you are found;
Or the one that is always around.
The truth will be revealed,
But it is by chance that the former will be sealed.

Surety has wandered.
Fate is not that of this earth;

It is in the love of all things true.
My soul is wide awake for you to view.
As the sun and moon share the morning sky,
Our peace can be found in the mind's eye.

Taming the Fire

You grab a hold of all my static and place all my
particles perfectly where they are preordained.
The way you budge piques my interest.
You stimulate me in a way that evokes emotion.

I am not biased.

Just when I feel myself begin to lose control,
A fire burns bright of orange and red embers,
I remain cautious as not to give in.
But you still find a way to make me melt.

(/) Drugs (/)

Oh, how I hate what you have taken,
Leaving behind the lifeless.
Strength is forsaken,
For the pain caused seems to be silenced.

I want you to stop, now!
You have taken the ones with bright smiles.My
family and friends are mine, for you I will not
endow.
Faith and strength are needed for these trials.

It is my mission,
to do as you have done to the innocent!
You have no power, it is in your execution
I will be vigilant.

For it is you I will ruin!
Love will win because it is something you do
not pursue in.

Love Thyself to The Moon & Back

You are that of a divine creation,
Do NOT live within the dictation.

They have created a dependent civilization.
This way of life disturbs the essential vibration.

Emotions are tossed and turned in the
gravitation,
For we yearn for the shifts of lunation.

Throughout the majestic rotation,
Societal life fills the soul with vexation.

Awaken thyself to our true formation.
It is a journey of love, not that of humation.

Explore yourself through mediation,
It is in the subconscious you may enjoy a bit of
liberation.

Don't Slip

You could blow it.
It's only present if you let it be.
I know sometimes I may just be lit,
But I promise it's you in my vision(s) that I see!
You not only become a part of me,
But you stand firmly with such grit.
God forbid,
I try to give you love for free;
At this rate, I don't know how I could ever quit.

Worn & Winkly

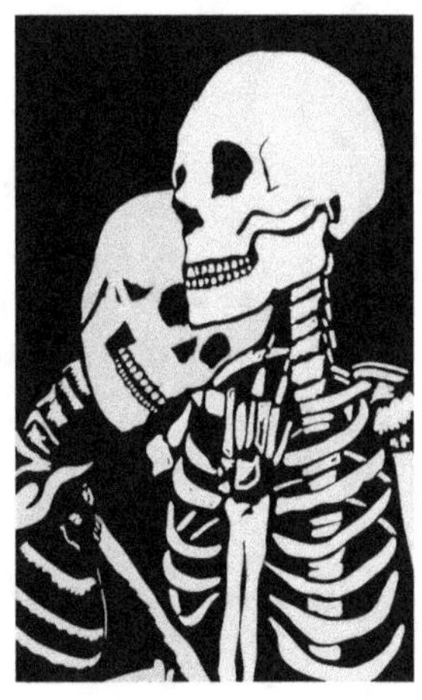

You don't reach out although smothered by
hands.
Admitting to the fear,
Is that of moral stance.
It is too toxic for you to remain near.

I crumple our compassion and hand it over,
Love in your heart has left.
You can not win at life by simply using a clover,
It hurts me to know we will end by a slow death.

Call me selfish, but I was taught to be a warrior.
I hope you realize it is love you deserve,
For with love change is loyal.

Motherhood is my stop, but remember what we
have learned...

32

www.ingramcontent.com/pod-product-compliance
Lightning Source LLC
Chambersburg PA
CBHW071235140726
47996CB00007B/2611